WORLD WAR II
PRELUDE TO WAR

WORLD WAR II
PRELUDE TO WAR

Published by Bookmart Ltd 2005

Blaby Road,
Wigson,
Leicester,
LE18 4SE
Books@bookmart.co.uk

All notations of errors or omissions (author inquiries, permissions) concerning the content of this book should be addressed to TAJ Books 27, Ferndown Gardens, Cobham, Surrey, UK, KT11 2BH, info@tajbooks.com.

ISBN 1-84509-166-3

Printed in China.
1 2 3 4 5 08 07 06 05

Contents

Adolf Hitler with his fellow Nazi party members.

The Warning

On 25 January 1938, the last year in the reign of Pope Pius XI, two months before the Anschluss, or German annexation of Austria, an eerie light was seen in many parts of Europe, reaching as far south as Rome. Unexplained forest and building fires were also reported. Twenty-one years earlier, in 1917, three children from an obscure village called Fatima in the centre of Portugal had testified to a number of messages of world consequence given to them by none other than Mary, the Mother of Jesus Christ. One of these messages had warned that: "World War I will end soon. However, if humanity does not stop offending God, another, and worse war will break out in the reign of Pius XI." The sign for this impending war was to be "a night illuminated by an unknown light".

However one wishes to interpret these strange events, and whether or not historians can agree that 1938 was the real beginning of World War II, containing as it did not only the Anschluss but the Munich crisis and the directive to the Wehrmacht for the final liquidation of Czecho-Slovakia, one thing can be certain: that World War II was indeed "worse" than its predecessor, World War I, which had been described as "the war to end war".

What immediately stands out from the casualty figures of the two world wars is that in World War II more civilians were killed than combatants, including well over five million Jews. The total of those who died in World War I was 8,538,315, while in World War II the military deaths on both sides in Europe alone numbered 19 million in contrast to six million in the war against Japan. In Poland 5,300,000 civilians died in addition to 120,000 combatants. A third of the civilian casualties were Jews.

Germany's Strengths

The build-up to World War II was characterised by the bullishness of the National Socialists and their skilful use of propaganda to compensate for areas of weakness. Their cause was aided by the reluctance of the major Western powers to confront them. That a powerful state with modern armaments like Czechoslovakia could have been absorbed by the Germans with barely a shot being fired demonstrated the true price of appeasement. Moreover, although sound defensive tactics had been enough to eventually turn the tide in the Allies favour in World War I, new circumstances and developments in tactics and armaments now favoured the aggressor. Men like General Heinz Guderian had been quick to take up new ideas on tank tactics which, although conceived by British thinkers such as Basil Liddell Hart, were rejected by conservative forces in the British high command. Thus the Germans developed the doctrine of the tank division used in conjunction with motorized artillery, motorised infantry divisions and dive bombers. The result was the "blitzkrieg" that literally took Europe by storm.

Naval Warfare

Although on the back foot militarily in 1939, Britain could still rely on naval ascendancy to keep it from disaster. What the Germans lacked by way of a powerful surface fleet was compensated for to some extent by the effectiveness of U-Boat

German U-Boauts in submarine pens, Norway.

Nazi rally in preparation for war, 1935.

German Stuka dive bomber.

German paratroopers invade Holland.

tactics, enhanced by strategic Atlantic ports. But partly due to Hitler's reluctance to commit resources to U-Boat development and partly due to improved convoy tactics and increasing aid from the U.S.A., the tide began to turn in the Allies favour.

Mercurial German surface raiders occasionally slipped out like sharks from their lairs, notably the Admiral Graf Von Spee, which was famously cornered by British cruisers at the Battle of the River Plate, and the Bismarck which, tracked down by almost the entire British Home Fleet, spectacularly sank that emblem of British naval power, H.M.S. Hood, before meeting its own grisly end in the Atlantic. In the clash with Bismarck the Royal Navy launched from H.M.S. Victorious its first ever aircraft-carrier strike against a German battleship at sea. Although this barely caused a dent, a second strike from H.M.S. Ark Royal was enough to damage the rudder and allow pursuing battleships to catch up.

The most spectacular entrance for aircraft-carrier tactics in World War II, however, was made by the Japanese at Pearl Harbor on 7 December 1941. Thereafter the aircraft carrier superseded the battleship as the dominant vessel of the war. The U.S.A. demonstrated even greater command of carrier tactics at Midway Island, Coral Sea and Leyte Gulf.

Air Power

In 1939, the Germans could hold their own in terms of the quantity of aircraft produced and the quality was second to none.

Russian tank on the move during the Battle of Kursk.

The Luftwaffe had also had the opportunity to practise air-to-ground support techniques in Spain. These tactics were anathema to senior British airmen and were only effectively employed by the British in 1942. Despite this, in the summer and autumn of 1940 the Royal Air Force achieved a victory over the Germans in the Battle of Britain which has become legendary. Here were knights of the air fighting the forces of evil over a land bathed in summer sunshine. Even the weapons they employed in the battle, notably the Supermarine Spitfire, seemed to be inspired.

After the Battle of Britain, it became apparent that the Germans, although starting the war with an impressive line up of aircraft, had made few plans for replacements in future years. By 1940, Britain alone was producing aircraft faster than Germany, and with the addition of U.S.A. resources, not to mention those of the Soviet Union, the imbalance in this vital arm of warfare became critical for Germany. By D-Day, the Germans had only 319 aircraft in the west against 12,837 for the Allies.

That the U.S.A. was in a position in 1945 not only to drop two atomic bombs on Japan more or less unopposed as well as launching raids as devastating as the Tokyo "fire raid" of 9 March 1945 shows to what extent Japanese air power, despite the excellence of fighters such as the Zero, had been eroded.

It was fortunate for the Western Allies that Hitler decided to turn on his erstwhile ally, the Soviet Union, and thus create a powerful enemy in the east that would eventually prove to be his Nemesis. In addition to the weapons they were able to supply from their own factories, the Soviets also had the advantage of a massive supply of equipment from the Western powers. By the end of 1943, in the wake of epic battles such as Stalingrad and Kursk, the Germans had lost two thirds of the territory they had taken. By April 1945 the Red Army had reached Berlin. The major role the Soviet Union had played in defeating Nazi Germany, however, was now to be sullied by the institution of anti-democratic communist regimes in Eastern Europe.

Balance of Power

Japan's spectacular assault on the U.S. Navy and Hitler's decision to declare war upon the U.S.A. brought into the equation a country that was not only the most powerful nation in the world but which was more powerful at the end of the war than at the beginning. From now on the Allies could rely on steadily achieving their objectives through what Winston Churchill described as "the proper application of overwhelming force". In the West the U.S. factories were producing massive amounts of armaments and even in the East the Soviets had succeeded in moving whole factories from under German noses to the safety of their vast hinterlands. At the Battle of Kursk the Soviet Union was able to field 4,000 vehicles to the Germans' 2,700. The fundamental superiority in training of the German soldier and the excellence of German staff officers and NCOs could not make up for the growing imbalance in resources. The Axis powers were also increasingly over-stretched and out-manouvred in the Intelligence game.

Whereas the Germans were often at the mercy of flawed decisions made during the volatile mood swings of their supreme commander, the Japanese desire to fight to the death meant that they failed to take the opportunity to devise more effective tactics on the ground. With the dropping of the two atomic bombs and the end of the war, the U.S.A. and the Soviet Union were the undisputed world powers, while Britain, although a victor and in command of much of its Empire, was bled white economically and at the end of an era in its history. Whereas Germany and Japan, despite being occupied, had no choice but to start completely afresh and begin to build powerful new economies, and whereas France succeeded in taking the initiative in European political experiments, Britain found itself caught between roles and with divided loyalties. The message at the end of World War II was this: that if there was to be another, even worse war, it would probably mean the end of humanity. Man's technological genius had made the prospect unthinkable.

Declaration of War - President Franklin D Roosewlt delivers message to congress.

June 28, 1914, Archduke Franz Ferdinand and his wife, the Duchess of Hohenberg, leave the town hall at Sarajevo. In a short time they will be dead and the inexorable slide to war will start.

The reasons for war

When WWI finally broke out, no one was surprised—it had been brewing for so long that a full-scale conflict was more or less inevitable. The actual trigger which started the war was the assassination of Archduke Franz Ferdinand in Sarajevo on June 28 1914. There were so many other factors involved, however, that even if the heir to the Austro-Hungarian throne had not been murdered it would have only been a matter of time before some other event initiated war.

The years leading up to the outbreak of war in 1914 were a time of rising nationalism in most of the major European countries of the day. As a result there were a lot of very aggressive leaders vying with each other for economic and imperial supremacy. This created an atmosphere of severe political tension—it was clear that war was the most likely outcome of the policies being followed.

One of the primary causes was that there were simply too many over-zealous people competing for the same foreign territories. The Industrial Revolution of the 19th century had seen a massive rise in the manufacturing power of many of the leading European powers, and their industries needed large markets to survive. Foremost in these were Great Britain, Germany, and France, and as their manufacturing centers produced more and more goods, their domestic markets were quickly swamped—the only way for them to continue expanding was through increasing the amount of goods exported.

Where there had once been enough third-world land for all the European countries to build their own empires, by the end of the nineteenth century there was very little left to claim. This meant that the only way to sustain imperial expansion was to capture land from someone else's empire. The African continent was the main area of dispute, and although Great Britain and France had many problems, they were at least able to resolve them diplomatically. This was not true of Germany, however, which clashed with both British and French interests in North Africa. To make matters even more combustible, the Ottoman Empire in the Middle East was falling apart. This made it a tempting target to the Austro-Hungarians, the Russians and to the various power-hungry leaders in the Balkans. As a consequence of this situation, many countries set up mutual alliances to try and ensure that they were not too vulnerable to attack from aggressive neighbors. As the various elements jostled for position, a vast arms race began.

As the military machines ground into action, many long-held national resentments also came to the fore. Several of these were rooted in the terms of the Congress of Vienna, which was held in 1815 at the end of the Napoleonic War. At this time Germany and Italy had been left as fragmented countries in order to help prevent another war starting. Italy, however, reunited in 1861 following the rise of nationalist movements, and Germany followed suit ten years later in 1871. To make matters worse, the Franco-Prussian War of 1870-71 had resulted in France losing the Alsace-Lorraine region to Germany; this had left the French people with a seething resentment and a strong desire for revenge.

When Bismarck formed the Three Emperor's League in 1872, it was a deliberate attempt to isolate the French to help ensure that they were not strong enough to start another major war. The alliance was between Germany, Russia and Austria-Hungary. This pact was then followed in 1882 by another called the "Triple Alliance"—it was formed between Germany, Italy and Austria-Hungary, and was a response to France occupying Tunisia. It played on Italy's fears over French aggression—in exchange for agreeing to remain neutral if a war broke out between Austria-Hungary and Russia, Germany and Austria-Hungary agreed to protect Italy from France.

The Balkans were also a melting pot of trouble—due to the diverse origins of its people, the region had a long history of conflict. In the pre-WWI era, both the Russians and the Austro-Hungarians had aspirations to incorporate the region into their empires, and so tensions between these two super-powers were high. Bismarck once again managed to create a pact in 1887

German field gun.

to ensure a short-term peace—this was called the "Reinsurance Treaty," and it basically stated that both sides would remain neutral in the event of the other going to war.

Although Bismarck had managed to create a series of alliances which helped to stabilize Eastern Europe for several years, he was fired by Kaiser William II in 1890. After he went, the pact with Russia was not renewed, and France quickly stepped in with the Franco-Russian Entente in 1891; this was formalized into an alliance in 1894. France and Great Britain had a common mistrust of Germany's ambitions, and decided that their best interests would be served by the creation of an alliance. They consequently set aside their colonial differences, and established the Entente Cordiale in 1904.

Germany's activities in the Balkans had meanwhile enraged the Russians, which pushed them into allying themselves with Great Britain by forming an Entente between the two countries in 1907. The new pact was then extended to include France by the formation of the Triple Entente. This effectively left Europe divided into two separate camps, between whom there was an increasing amount of tension.

Although Russia was the largest country involved, and Great Britain had the biggest navy, Germany had by far the strongest army. Since everyone was sure that war was inevitable, all the other countries began to strengthen their military machines. Large-scale conscription was implemented, and both France and

German light cruisers and destroyers manoeuvre in the Baltic.

Germany doubled the size of their armies between 1870 and 1914. Great Britain and Germany became very competitive over the sizes of their navies. It became an official mantra in Britain that it had to have a navy that was two and a half times larger than the nearest rival to maintain its naval superiority. In response to this new demand the Royal Navy built and launched the Dreadnought Class of battleship in 1906. Germany responded in kind by designing and building her own massive warships.

Although there were attempts to slow the arms race at the Hague Conferences in 1899 and 1907, there was little change in the determination of the countries concerned to lead the competition to stay ahead in military terms. Many technical changes were also made to both equipment and organizational methods. Not all these proved to be an asset in the long run, however. The planning structures some of the countries came up with often became so complicated that once a plan was put into action it proved almost impossible to change it. One victim of this was the von Schlieffen Plan, which was created by the German military command. This was a detailed organizational account which specified that France should be attacked in the event of Germany going to war with Russia. It was a needlessly

German light cruisers manoeuvre in the Baltic.

complicated affair with a momentum that proved to be hard to control.

The mounting tension in Europe made itself felt in many places around the world. In 1905, Morocco was supported in its call for independence by Germany. Although it had been a British colony for some time, it had been handed over to France in 1904. When the crisis arose, Great Britain stood up for France against Germany, and war was only avoided when an international conference was held in Algeciras in 1906. This allowed France to turn Morocco into a French protectorate.

Just as the Moroccan conflict was settled, a new one arose—this time in the Balkans. Once again, it was the work of the German / Austro-Hungarian governments, and was caused by their annexation of Bosnia—a former Turkish province, by Austria-Hungary in 1908. Things were extremely tense during this period as their actions nearly started a war with Russia. Serbia had its sights set on taking Bosnia for itself, and so its people were infuriated when the country was snatched from their grasp by the Austro-Hungarians. Serbia threatened to start a war over the affair, and as it had aligned itself with Russia, a large-scale mobilization began. In the end the Russians were persuaded to back down, but relations between all the countries concerned were increasingly strained from then on.

In 1911, a second Moroccan crisis blew up when Germany claimed that France had violated the terms of the Algeciras Agreement. A German warship was sent to Agadir, however, Great Britain once again stood up for France and in the end an agreement was reached whereby Germany was given part of the French Congo.

Just as the second Moroccan crisis was settled, war broke out in the Balkans in 1912. The Balkan States drove the Turks out of the area and back as far as Constantinople—they then set about fighting amongst themselves over exactly who got which territories. While this was going on, Austria-Hungary took some of the new land Serbia had acquired, raising tensions even further. This stirred some of the Serbian Nationalists up to fever pitch. On June 28, 1914, they struck back when a Serbian nationalist belonging to the secret Black Hand (Narodna Obrana) organization managed to assassinate the Archduke Francis Ferdinand, heir to the Austria-Hungarian throne in Sarajevo, Bosnia. Austria-Hungary chose to blame the Serbian government for the killing, even though it was almost certainly nothing to do with them; this stance was strongly backed by Germany. As a result, Austria-Hungary made unreasonable territorial and political demands of the Serbians, and even though they agreed to the terms, a declaration of war was made against Serbia on July 28, 1914.

Over the next few days a series of threats and counter-threats resulted in an unstoppable path to war. The day after Austria-Hungary declared war, Russia mobilized to support Serbia, and on July 31, Germany stated that if Russia did not demobilize, she would go to war against her as well. In the meantime France also mobilized, this time in support of Russia. The imminent Balkan conflict actually became the start of the first global war when Germany declared war on Russia on August 1, 1914. On August 3, France declared war on Germany, which then responded by breaking through the borders of Belgium in order to reach Paris by the shortest route. In doing this, Germany violated a country which had been officially neutral until then. This brought Great Britain into the war when King Albert I of Belgium appealed to the British for help on August 4, 1914, and four years of bitter conflict were underway.

On hearing the news that war had broken out, President Woodrow Wilson immediately declared that the United States was neutral. In stark contrast, Japan declared war on Germany on August 23, 1914, in accordance with a military agreement with Great Britain. Austria-Hungary then responded two days later by declaring war on Japan. Italy managed to avoid joining the war even though it had an agreement to defend both Germany and Austria-Hungary against aggressors. It's claim was that the arrangement was only valid in the event of either country being attacked—she stated that as they were doing the attacking, there was no obligation for her to participate. In order to avoid being drawn in by either side, Italy initially declared herself neutral, but was eventually persuaded to join the Allies in May 1915.

The Russian Tsar accompanied by Grand-Duke Nicholas salutes as he inspects his troops.

The War

When the war got underway in August 1914, there were several different countries on each side. The Germans and Austro-Hungarians were joined by the Bulgarians and the Turks along with the remnants of the Ottoman Empire. Against them were ranged the forces of Great Britain, Russia, Italy, France, Belgium, Serbia, Montenegro and Japan. A year before the end of the war the United States also entered the fray.

The conflict in the west actually began shortly after war was declared between France and Germany on August 3, 1914, with German armies invading Belgium at great speed as they made their way towards Paris. This highly mobile attack had been a principle component in what was known as the Schlieffen Plan, which also intended for the French Armies to be encircled and destroyed. Liege fell on August 7, and the invading armies continued on their way with all the speed they could muster. By August 18, the First, Second, Third, Fourth and Fifth armies were in position to encircle the defending forces, and on August 20, the Sixth and Seventh armies under the command of Crown Prince Rupprecht of Bavaria took on the French who had moved into the Upper Alsace region. They soon drove the French back to their border fortifications, however, the would-be invaders were stopped short by this range of substantial fortresses.

When the French tried to strike back in the German centre

north of Metz they were roundly defeated by the Fourth and Fifth armies on August 22–25. At much the same time, other German forces moved into northern France, taking victories from the French at Namur and the British at Mons over August 22–23. At this stage two army corps under Moltke's command were transferred to the eastern front by the German High Command to help with matters there. Shortly after this further forces were also moved to the Eastern Front, leaving only 40 of the original 52 divisions in the five northern armies. At first this was not a problem as progress was still being made, however, they then found that they no longer had the necessary strength to take Paris from the west as had been intended. By September 2, the First Army was positioned to the east of the city having pursued the retreating French forces for some time.

Although the German armies were trying to encircle the French, the defender's fortifications prevented them from breaking through the Moselle region. This resulted two days later in the German armies being strung out along a 125 mile-long front, from Meaux, 25 miles to the east of Paris, to an area to the southwest of Verdun. The commander of the French forces, General Joffre, then tried to strike back with 52 divisions whilst the Sixth Army under General Maunoury tried to outflank the right wing of the German lines held by the German First Army.

When the French First Army consisting of 150,000 troops, and the German Sixth Army confronted each other, a fierce battle broke out that lasted for three days. Although this conflict which

German troops in a defensive position during the battle of Tannenberg in East Prussia.

later became known as the First Battle of the Marne went in the favor of the Germans, its commander, Chief of Staff Helmuth von Moltke realized that things had not gone as well as initial reports had suggested, and that his forces were in a rather precarious position. In turning his forces to face the French, he left a large gap between his First Army and the neighboring Second Army. The British soldiers of the British Expeditionary Force quickly drove through the gap along with French troops from the Fifth Army. Meanwhile the French Sixth Army, bolstered by fresh reserves, managed to hold off the German attack.

Moltke had made a poor decision in trying to control his armies from a position that was a long way back from the front. His communication lines proved to be far from satisfactory, and as a result he had a very poor grasp of the true situation on the battlefield. Fearing that the Allies were going to break through and encircle his forces, he ordered a retreat. The Allies failed to make the most of the withdrawal, and as a result the German armies were able to dig in and prepare substantial defences after retreating only 40 miles. This temporary network of trenches north of the River Aisne ended up marking the front line for the next four years.

The Battle of the Marne marked the failure of the Schlieffen Plan and as such ended all German hopes for a fast invasion of France. It also showed that the Allies were capable of standing up to the might of the German army. The human cost of the battle was astonishing, with the French losing around 250,000 men, and the Germans a similar number; the British Expeditionary Force listed 12,733 casualties. The German chief of staff, Helmuth

British Royal Marines landed at Ostend August 27-28, 1914.

von Moltke also became a casualty as shortly after the retreat he suffered a major breakdown, and was replaced by General Erich von Falkenhayn. Things were not going well on the Eastern Front either, with the Russian commander in chief, Grand Duke Nicholas sending twenty-eight divisions to invade East Prussia from the east and south to help relieve the pressure on the French. This tied up German forces that would have otherwise been able to help support those fighting the Allies on the Western Front.

Not long after the Germans had dug themselves in to their trench defence system, the Allies rushed to attack them before they could regroup for a second attack on Paris. The British Expeditionary Force managed to retake Ypres, a small medieval town in Belgium, from the Germans. When they tried to take it back, the consequent battle lasted from October 31–November 17, 1914, and became known as the First Battle of Ypres. The

BEF 60-pounder.

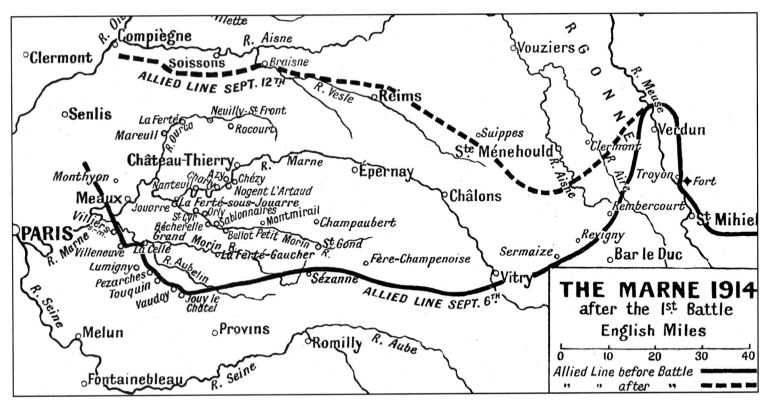

Map showing the battle of the Marne between 6 and 12 September; the battle saved Paris and halted the German advance.

British troops maintained their lines against sustained attacks, but suffered very heavy casualties. Just as it looked as though they would not be able to hold on, the French sent reinforcements, and the German attack was called off.

Although things had gone badly for the German Army after its first four months of fighting on the Western Front, the same could not be said of its affairs on the Eastern Front. The Austro-Hungarian army, however, had taken terrible losses in its attempts to take Serbia. It lost some 300,000 troops killed, injured or taken prisoner at the Battle of Lemberg. This eradicated the elite of the Austro-Hungarian officer corps, a tragedy from which the country never fully recovered. The battle had also proved costly for the Russians though, and this made it impossible for Grand Duke Nicholas to mount his intended attack on Berlin.

The Germany Army fared somewhat better than their neighbors, and their conflict with the Russians escalated until a four day battle began on August 26 at Tannenberg. In this action, 166,000 German troops commanded by Erich Ludendorff and Paul von Hindenburg achieved the greatest victory of the war on the Eastern front. They faced 200,000 opponents, and succeeded in taking 92,000 Russian prisoners, killing or injuring most of the others. By the middle of the following month, most of East Prussia was back in German hands.

All this took a terrific toll on German resources, however,

German generals and the Kaiser.

and after their defeat at Marne, the German minister of war, Falkenhayn, was thoroughly disillusioned. He came to the belief that if Germany had to fight England, France, and Russia at the same time, she could not possibly win. If the conflict became a contest of attrition, Germany would not be able to hold on for ever.

As the war continued into 1915, Germany continued to fight on two main fronts. In the west "total war" was declared, and in January German Zeppelin airships bombed England and killed large numbers of civilians. This was followed in February by the start of a submarine blockade of Britain. Although Germany declared that any ship approaching Britain was a legitimate target, the United States issued Germany with a stern warning not to kill any American citizens. Fighting continued on both the Eastern and Western Fronts, with the Battle of Neuve Chapelle taking place from March 10–13. This resulted in a small territorial gain for the British, but at a terrible human cost.

In April, the Allies began a battle for the Turkish peninsula of Gallipoli, an action that was to last for nine-months and consume large quantities of badly needed resources. This considerably reduced the effectiveness of their forces fighting on the Western Front. The same month the Germans launched the Second Battle of Ypres, which began with an artillery barrage that was followed

German troops using machine guns in open country as they slowly creep forward.

by the first ever poison gas attack, with yellow clouds of mustard gas drifting back and forth across the lines, killing and injuring troops on both sides. The battle which followed took another massive toll of human lives.

On May 7, a German U-boat torpedoed a British ship—the Lusitania; this resulted in the deaths of 1,198 civilians, of which 128 were Americans. This infuriated the United States, and made relations with Germany extremely tense. At the end of August, Germany—increasingly worried that America might enter the war on the side of the Allies, agreed to stop sinking ships without warning. Meanwhile, on the Eastern Front, command of the

Russian armies was taken over by Tsar Nicholas on September 5. In mid-December, command of the British Expeditionary Force fighting on the Western Front was taken over by Sir Douglas Haig. At the end of the month the Allies decided that there was no longer any hope of sustaining the fight for Gallipoli, and they began withdrawing troops from the peninsula.

The Allies' desperate need for fresh troops eventually forced the British government to introduce conscription, and on February 10, 1916, the conscription law was put into effect. Later the same month the Battle of Verdun began. This was to become the longest battle of the war, and it lasted until December 18, with an estimated cost of one million lives. At the end of the conflict there was no clear winner. While the fight for Verdun was

Clouds of German poison gas drift towards Russian lines.

German U-boat demands the surrender of a British merchant ship.

being waged, the war continued elsewhere. On May 15, Vimy Ridge—a key geographical feature, was taken by the Canadians. Over May 31–June 1 the only major naval engagement of the war was fought at the Battle of Jutland. Although massive naval artillery barrages were fired by both sides, there was no clear winner. In July the Allies launched the Battle of the Somme—this was to prove to be another long, drawn-out conflict which resulted in enormous numbers of casualties. It is estimated that between July 1 and November 18, around one million troops were killed or injured, after which time the Allies had failed to make the breakthrough they had planned. During this time the Allies introduced the first tanks. Although they proved to be an

effective weapon, there were far too few of them to make any real difference to the course of the battle.

On February 1, 1917, the Germans re-started their campaign of unrestricted submarine warfare, angering the Americans sufficiently to bring them to the edge of declaring war on Germany. The following month Tsar Nicholas II of Russia abdicated, and a provisional government was declared. This had little immediate effect on the state of affairs on the Eastern Front, however, this situation was not to last long. On April 6,, President Wilson went before the American Congress and asked for a declaration of war with Imperial Germany.

Later the same month the French launched what was probably the most abortive battle of the entire war at Chemin des Dames.

French troops in early 1915.

German machine gunners in Poland, 1915.

In this disastrous offensive which lasted from April 16–29 they only managed to advance 500 yards with a tragic cost of over 250,000 casualties. After this appalling waste of human lives, more than half a million French troops mutinied and refused to carry on with the senseless attempt to take a few more yards of unimportant ground.

In May, the United States government further prepared to enter the war in Europe by passing a law allowing it to draft men into the armed forces. The first contingent of American troops actually landed in France on July 3, as the advance party of the much larger American Expeditionary Force. While fresh soldiers were being shipped across the Atlantic to assist in the war on the Western Front, things were going very badly for the Russians over on the Eastern Front. The catastrophic performance of the Imperial Russian Army over the duration of the war had demoralized the troops, and many had simply refused to fight on. In an attempt to turn the tide of the war the head of the provisional government, Alexander Kerensky led a major offensive in Galicia, however, as civil war swept through Russia, the Germans struck back and the assault collapsed in total disarray. On November 7, Kerensky's government was overthrown by Bolshevik socialists, led by Lenin. Less than a month later Leon Trotsky, representing the new Russian government, signed an armistice with Germany. The final outcome of this was a settlement known as the Treaty of Brest-Litovsk.

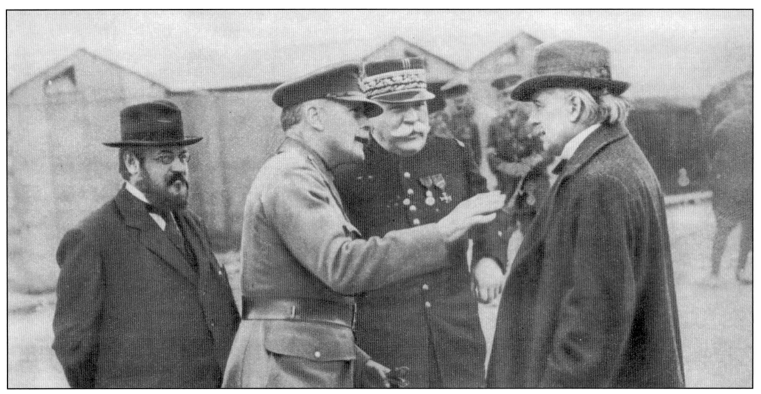

From left to right: French Minister of Munitions, Albert Thomas; Sir Douglas Haig; General Joffre; Lloyd George who was British Minister of Munitions and then Secretary for War.

Although American troops were arriving in Europe from the beginning of July, they were not battle-ready, and had to undergo considerable amounts of further training and resupply. While this was going on, the Allies launched the Third Battle of Ypres, a massive offensive which is usually referred to as Passchendaele. This began on July 31, and lasted until November 10. Although the aims of the attack made strategic sense, the end result was that once again very little changed on the territorial map. The toll on human lives, however, was appalling, with some 700,000 casualties overall.

As the winter of 1917/1918 drew to a close, it became clear to the German high command that their forces would not be able to match the might of the huge numbers of American troops that were now being readied for war. In an attempt to win the war before these fresh troops appeared in the trenches, the German Army launched the first of five major offensives on March 21, 1918. Although the advances were initially successful, British and Australian troops managed to stop the German advance near Amiens on April 25. Two days later, the first significant American involvement in the war took place when the 1st U.S. Division took up positions in the region North of Paris. Towards the end of May, however, the Germans had got close enough to Paris for their larger guns to be able to shell the city. Things then began to improve for the Allies, and on May 31, American troops at

King Ferdinand of Bulgaria in consultation with General Ivanoff.

Chateau-Thierry prevented German forces from crossing the Marne.

Although the fact that American troops were now fighting was yet to have a major effect on the course of the war, it did help demoralize the German troops who were being shipped across Europe from the Eastern to the Western Fronts. Large numbers of these battle-weary soldiers simply jumped off their transport trains and deserted. In August, the Allies mounted a major counter offensive on the Somme, and managed to force the Germans into a hasty retreat. This was followed by the Battle of St. Mihiel, which lasted from September 12–16, where American troops fought independently for the first time. Up until this point they had only fought as part of the French forces, but General John Pershing, Commander of the American Expeditionary Force had insisted on taking charge of his own battlefront sector. Once freed of foreign control, he was able to set about doing things his own way.

One of Pershing's top commanders was a young officer called Colonel George S. Patton Jr., who would later rise to world-wide fame during WWI. He set his units up such that once the battle had started they could function without further orders. This was a fundamental change from the entrenched system used by the British, French and German armies. The freedom to respond to changes in the battlefield situation without having to wait an age for the chain of command to issue new orders was a major step

German storm troopers on the Eastern Front holding a shallow line of pits before advancing.

forward. One of the most significant examples of this was in the way they used armor. Pershing had been so impressed with how the British uses tanks that he created small armored platoons that operated without infantry support. These units were able to drive Germans troops back further and faster than had ever been achieved before.

The Battle of St. Mihiel, which lasted from September 12–16, 1918, was not only notable in terms of the first independent operation of American troops, but also because it was the biggest air battle the world had ever seen. Around 1,476 allied aircraft—made up from the air forces of the U.S., France, Italy,

Great Britain and Portugal, were used to provide ground cover for the troops in the trenches. Facing them were 500 or so German planes, the destruction of which was a primary Allied goal. When the battle commenced, the objectives were quickly achieved, and the German troops fell back in disarray. Nine days after the Battle of St. Mihiel, the German front was breached at the Hindenburg line, and Allied troops broke through. It was clear that the Allies were now strong enough to push all the way forward into Germany itself. On October 28, German sailors demonstrated their feelings on their chances when they were ordered to fight a naval battle they had no chance of winning. Instead of needlessly sacrificing their lives, they mutinied whilst still in port. On October 30, the Turks ended their part in the war when they signed an armistice. A few days later, on November 9, Kaiser Wilhelm II realized that all was lost, and he abdicated. The next day a German republic was founded, and on November 11, at 11 o'clock on the 11th day of the 11th month of 1918, the war finally ended as Germany and the Allies signed an Armistice.

In the aftermath of the war there were many lessons to be learned. For a start, the Germans had not responded to changes in the way war was conducted as a result of advances in technology. While long command chains were all very well for battlefields full of cavalry, they had been completely outmoded. The highly responsive command methods employed by the Americans in the closing stages of the war had proved very effective, to the detriment of the German armies. This phase of the war was closely studied over the next few years, and the conclusions drawn were used as the seeds of a new form of warfare based around rapid mobility. At the beginning of WWII this quickly became known to the rest of the world as Blitzkrieg.

Another important lesson learned by both the Germans and the Allies was that Great Britain was vulnerable to submarine blockades. While it had been easy top keep the German surface fleet trapped in their ports, their U-boat submarines had operated with relative impunity. This factor was exploited to the maximum in WWII, and had it not been for new methods of fighting submarines, could well have forced a different outcome.

The human cost of WWI was astonishing, with around nine million people killed or injured in the fighting. To make matters worse, however, the end of the war also saw an outbreak of influenza that killed more people world-wide than the four

years of WWI. The long-term effects, however, were far more insidious, for the way the war ended became a major factor in the start of WWII. The reasons for this are many and varied, but in essence, when the war ended the German people felt betrayed rather than defeated. Although Allied troops had indeed beaten their armies, foreign soldiers had never set foot on German soil, and so the populace felt distanced from the action. They had no understanding of the mathematics of attrition, or of the might of the combined armies and industrial output of the Allied partners. When the end came, they only saw the politicians giving in and the harsh effects on the nation of the Treaty of Versailles. This limited the German army to a maximum of 100,000 troops and blamed Germany for starting the war—as a consequence of this, she had to pay massive reparations. It also gave Western Prussia to Poland, and Alsace-Lorraine to France. These penalties instilled in the German people a feeling of frustration, anger, and of humiliation. The national economy suffered as a result, and large numbers of people lost their jobs and livelihoods. The next decade would prove to be a harsh time for Germany, and these deeply-held resentments were cleverly exploited by Adolf Hitler as he sought to achieve power. Consequently, the path to the next war was neatly laid.

The Unknown Warrior's coffin resting in Westminster Abbey, in London, November 9, 1920. The carnage of World War I left most Europeans prepared to do anything to stop another war.

The sudden end of World War I came as a shock to the German people—not only had they unexpectedly lost the war itself, but the national economy was in turmoil and the political situation was dire. In October 1918 Soldiers and sailors had mutinied in their home barracks, and workers had formed militant union councils. Within two weeks there was revolution and a republic was claimed. This caused the abdication of the Kaiser, which marked the end of the Hohenzollern dynasty. In its wake came a military dictatorship led by Erich Ludendorff and Paul von Hindenburg. On November 11, Armistice was declared and World War I came to an abrupt end.

On January 18, 1919, the Paris Peace Conference began, and the allies were in no mood to let the Germans off lightly. The price exacted for Germany going to war was not only financial, but geographical. This was partly in recompense for the massive loses suffered, but was also an attempt to stabilize the area to foster a long-lasting peace in Europe. The result of the reparations imposed was that the German economy collapsed—inflation spread like wild-fire, and those who had their life savings held in bank accounts lost everything.

A new German National Assembly was elected on January 19, 1919, but because Berlin was suffering from riots and other violent disorders, they met for the first time in Weimar. This new government was in fact a coalition of the three main parties—the SPD, DDP, and Center under the chancellorship of Philipp Scheidemann. Shortly after this the National Assembly elected Friedrich Ebert (SPD) to be the first President of the Republic.

While the allies argued to and fro over the terms of the

French soldiers waiting in front of the Versailles castle for the signature of the Treaty of Versailles.

peace settlement, Germany's mainstream politics were in a state of disarray. Having been ruled by the Kaiser and his dynasty for many generations, the new political parties were still very immature, and the Socialists suffered from factional power plays which threatened their very survival. Chief amongst the radical elements were the Spartacists, who were for outright communism and supported Lenin and the Bolsheviks—they wanted a full radical revolution, and brought about a series of major public disorders in an attempt to bring down the government of the elected President, Friedrich Ebert. Mid-way between the radicals and the middle of the road socialists were the

M. Clemenceau, the French Prime Minister, leaving the Chateau at Versailles after the Peace Treaty had been signed, January 1, 1919.

Independent Socialists who operated by organizing all manner of demonstrations, strikes, and putsches, and were not at all interested in maintaining the status quo.

As a result of these threats to the government, Ebert was forced to turn to the army for direct support, which he achieved by reaching agreement with General Wilhelm Groener. To back this up, Ebert then got one of his Socialist colleagues, Gustav Noske, to create a paramilitary unit called the Free Corps (Freikorps). This force was supported by the army, and provided the much needed muscle that was desperately needed to suppress the violence that the radicals were using on the streets throughout Germany.

The Spartacists tried to move on the government by taking Berlin, but the Free Corps went into action and secured many of the key strategic positions before eventually defeating them. The two main Spartacist leaders were captured and executed, and German politics settled down once again.

While the establishment of a new government may have given the German people some comfort, the allies were still working out the level of reparations they were going to impose. In April 1919, a figure of £5.4 billion was proposed—this was a staggering sum for the time. There was still much resentment amongst the German military, and when they realized that they were going to have to hand over their navy to the allies, they scuttled their entire fleet at Scapa Flow in June 1919, days before the Versailles Treaty was signed.

One of the biggest obstacles the treaty had to overcome in finding a permanent solution to the troubles in the region was

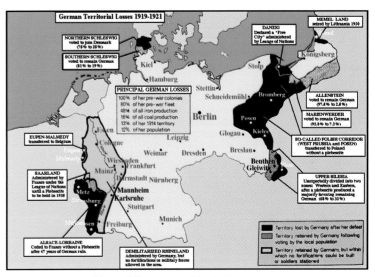

German territorial losses following World War I.

that Germany and France were not only situated next to each other, they had a history of fighting each other stretching back into the mists of time. The most prosperous area in the Franco-German borders lay along the route of the River Rhine—this was not only significant for trade, but also for strategic purposes. The river itself is so large that it has been a natural defence line for thousands of years. For an army to cross it without using bridges would be a major task, and so the French were keen to see the Rhineland become a natural buffer to German aggression. France also had designs on Germany's steel and coal industries in the area which had a far greater output than her own. It was proposed that an independent state was created to achieve this, and as with any territorial dispute, there were native inhabitants both for and against the idea. When it came to the crunch, however, even with the French offering a "no reparations" settlement, the separatists were too few in number for it to work.

When it came on June 28, 1919, the Versailles Treaty was a

New York greets the news of the Armistice.

Although almost obliterated by enemy bombardments, Ypres was the only important Belgian town not to fall to the Germans, despite being the scene of three of the costliest battles of the war. Postwar the city would have to be completely rebuilt.

A happy crowd in Paris wave the Stars and Stripes and the French flag.

devastating blow to Germany—it had to hand over large amounts of territory to its neighbors. Poland took the Polish Corridor and Silesia, France got the Alsace-Lorraine region, and other areas were given to Belgium and Denmark. Something else that sowed the seeds of bitter resentment in many people was that Germany was not allowed to unite with Austria. In order to reduce the possibility of Germany becoming a military threat in the future, its army was also limited to a maximum of 100,000 men.

When France was given the Alsace-Lorraine region, it got Germany's Saar valley—the French coal mining industry had been all but completely destroyed during the war, and so they were given the Saar valley (which was a premier coal mining area) in recompense. Although they didn't manage to get an independent

The victorious Allies on the steps of Marshal Foch's special train in the forest of Compiègne where the Armistice was signed.

After 47 years under German rule the French cavalry are joyously greeted in Strasbourg.

state created, the French did get the concession that the Rhineland would be occupied by Allied troops for fifteen years—after which it would become a demilitarized zone. They also managed to get the Americans and British to make a guarantee that they would come to her aid should Germany try to invade France again.

Although it seemed that a settlement had been reached that would create sufficient stability for a long-lasting European peace, the power-brokers overlooked a vital factor—that the German people as a whole believed that they hadn't lost the war in the true military sense, but that instead they'd been betrayed by the politicians. Had Germany been occupied by invading troops, the people may have felt differently, but for the vast majority the end of the war came as a remote, anticlimactic event. It is not clear just how this feeling could have been overcome at the time, but in ignoring it, the politicians allowed a wound to fester, something that would return to haunt the world within twenty years.

On top of the geographical losses, Germany also had to make reparations payments of £1 billion, and was made less significant

A searchlight belonging to the French army of occupation on the Rhine opposite St. Goar.

Crowds cheer British cavalry as they enter Spa on November 28, 1919.

The German fleet was scuttled at Scapa Flow on June 21, 1919 (this is the Hindenburg). This would mean that the Nazis would have to start building a navy from scratch.

on the world political stage by being barred from the League of Nations. There were many reasons why the reparations favored France so heavily—having had their population decimated by the enormous human cost of the series of wars led by Napoleon, they could ill afford to fight another with Germany. On top of this, World War I killed off a large proportion of the males of fighting age, as well as significant numbers of civilians. Where once the two nations were of similar sizes, France now only had two thirds of Germany's population, which, to make matters worse was increasing at a dramatic rate. This meant that in the post-war era, the French had fallen a long way behind their aggressive neighbor in the power stakes, both militarily and economically.

While the French were doing their best to get the most out of the peace settlement, the Americans and British were concerned that France may end up too powerful, which would have been just as bad for stability as if Germany retained power. What was need was a balance, but this was not proving easy to establish.

As an immediate challenge to the power of the peace treaty, on September 12, 1919, a small Italian military force seized the town of Fiume—what is now the city of Rijeka on the Dalmatian coast. This small expeditionary force was led by a maverick who acted without authority. After ruling the town through martial law for a year, he was forced out when he became too much of an embarrassment to the Italian government. While this episode is almost insignificant when viewed at the global level, it did highlight the inadequacies of the existing regulatory system.

As a forerunner to the creation of the United Nations, the League of Nations was intended to engender world peace, however, in many ways it was little more than a political road-show. The first full meeting took place in January 1920, but every nation that belonged to it had the power of veto, and some of the biggest players, including America, refused to join. Consequently, any pacts made under its auspices were barely worth the paper they were written on. This left France in a tricky position—although there was a League of Nations guarantee of her safety, the French pushed for the Treaty of Versailles to include a clause to provide military backing should Germany threaten her borders again. While this may have seemed to settle France's security concerns, the American Congress couldn't agree on the terms of the treaty, and failed to sign up to it, leaving the matter unresolved.

Although the peace settlement had made the Rhineland a demilitarized zone, in April 1920 the German government sent troops in to the area to quell rioting—this infuriated the French, who then invaded the Ruhr themselves. A month later they withdrew under pressure from the Americans and British.

The final level of financial reparations still hadn't been set, and once the League of Nations got involved, they argued back and forth for more than a year. On April 25, 1920, a figure of £4.5 billion was proposed—this was lower than had been suggested a year earlier, and so was rejected. In June the figure was raised to £12.5 billion—this amount was totally impractical, and after another six months of argument it was lowered to £10 billion, but this still failed to be accepted. The German delegation dug their heels in to try and get the figure lowered considerably, and in March 1921 in desperation at the way things were going, British, French and Belgian troops invaded the Ruhr to force Germany to toe the line.

With the presence of an allied military force in the Rhineland, the German delegation was more amenable, and the sum for reparations was finally agreed by all concerned at £6.6 billion—to be paid in instalments until 1984. To make sure that the agreement was taken seriously, allied troops stayed in place until the end of September. To the common people, however, this occupation created a huge amount of resentment, and while the world players were virtually playing chess with the map of Europe, a then unheard of Adolf Hitler joined a small political party in Munich called the German Workers Party—this was later to become the National Socialist German Workers Party, or Nazi Party.

The four Allied leaders during the peace conference (left to right: Georges Clemenceau, French Prime Minister; Woodrow Wilson, U.S. President; Vittorio Orlando (partly hidden), Italian Prime Minister; David Lloyd George, British Prime Minister).

Hitler and Goebbels are greeted off an aircraft in the 1930s.

HITLER AND THE GROWTH OF THE NAZI PARTY

Hitler at a memorial to the fallen in Hiltpoltstein, northern Bavaria.

Just how Adolf Hitler became to be so influential in German politics needs some explanation; he was born on April 20, 1889—a sickly baby, he was doted on by his over-protective mother. His father, however, was an abusive tyrant, who made his childhood and teenage years very difficult. His stubborn will earned him many beatings from his father—this left him with a sense of repressed anger, something that in his adult years easily spilled over into dramatic rages.

In the early years of schooling, Hitler was a good pupil, but as things became more difficult at home, he turned into a lazy, disinterested student. The only person who could hold his attention was his history teacher, Dr. Leopold Poetsch, who was a fervent Pan-German nationalist. The Pan-Germans believed in the superiority of the Aryan race, and that the strength of the German culture came from a strong, healthy, rustic lineage. They also believed that the Jews were an inferior race, as were many of the other Eastern European peoples, such as the Slavs. Dr. Poetsch's beliefs had a huge influence on Hitler, and later these ideas became a main component in his political campaigns.

Hitler's laziness at school meant that he had a complete lack of qualifications when he left—he had ambitions of becoming an artist, but when he applied to the various arts academies in Vienna, he was told that he wasn't good enough and that he wasn't qualified. When his mother died in 1907, Hitler was grief stricken, and inconsolable. The combination of this loss with his repressed anger meant that he was now a very bitter young man. When he read that the Jews were scheming to destroy German culture and to achieve world domination, he believed every word.

Hitler and Hindenberg during the opening of the Reichstag March 21st 1933.

Hitler enjoying a break while electioneering in the Harz mountains.

He further read that they were in league with the Catholics, Freemasons, and Jehovah's Witnesses, which riled him. He began talking of these matters with his friends, and such was the mass appeal of the message, he soon found himself at the center of an admiring throng. He lapped up the attention, and started searching out more racist material to bolster his standing in this new social circle.

In 1914 Hitler was arrested for failing to register for military duty, but on medical screening was found to be too weak to bear arms, and so escaped service. His attitude seems to have changed after the Austrian Archduke Francis Ferdinand was assassinated, however, since he suddenly volunteered for military duty. In August he joined the 16th Bavarian Reserve Infantry Regiment, and saw his first action two months later, 5 miles east of Ypres. Shortly after this he was made a messenger to his unit's

The Obersalzberg in Bavaria was the location of Hitler's favourite hideaway—the Berghof. He first moved into a wooden farmhouse in 1925 but by the 1930s it had been completely rebuilt. These scenes show Hitler in casual clothing greeting locals, in conversation with Göring (below left) and talking to 'Ein Kamerad aus dem Feld'—a fellow soldier from the first war.

Hitler in the passenger seat of his Mercedes.

headquarters, but this didn't stop him being awarded the Iron Cross Second Class within a month.

The next couple of years were not particularly spectacular for Hitler; in 1915 he was made up to Lance Corporal, and in October 1916 he received a leg wound at the Somme, after which he spent two months in a military hospital near Berlin. He was wounded again in 1917, although it was only minor. When he returned to service, he saw action at Picardy, the Ypres Salient and at the infamous Passchendaele.

As the war drew to a close, he was awarded the Iron Cross First Class for his service as messenger a since 1914. Not long after this, his life was spared by a British soldier who couldn't bring himself to shoot a wounded man—this event was later seen by Hitler as a divine intervention that showed he was indeed fated to lead the world. A further incident that shaped his view of warfare—and ultimately worked in favor of the allies during World War II, was

Hitler's open-topped Mercedes.

Hitler flies to another rally.

that in October 1918, Hitler was gassed and temporarily blinded. This effected him both physically and emotionally—years later when he came to power he refused to allow gas to be used by his armed forces. This meant that for moral reasons the allies couldn't use chemical weapons either, leading to a very unnatural military situation. Had Hitler not had personal experience of the horrors of using gas on the battlefield, World War II would almost certainly have been conducted in a very different (and far more brutal) manner.

When Hitler heard news of the armistice, he reacted very bitterly, and looked to his own hatreds to provide answers. Although finding other people to blame was his way of dealing with his personal situation, he was far from alone, since the vast majority of the German people also wanted someone else to blame. From his distorted perspective, he could give them answers as to why they'd lost the war, why the economy had collapsed, and why the country was in political turmoil—the "Great Jewish Conspiracy" had became his banner.

On the Bückeberg during the 1934 Harvest Festival.

Hitler was a man of paradoxes—on the one hand he had shown himself to be lazy, arrogant and riddled with delusions of grandeur, but on the other hand he'd volunteered for military service, had been decorated for bravery, and never drank alcohol or smoked tobacco. On top of this he was a vegetarian who loved animals, and a hypochondriac who constantly worried about his health. In the post-Great War era, he found himself in the midst of all the political and economic uncertainty that was tearing Germany apart. It was into this climate of revolts, Putsch's and demonstrations that he now threw himself.

The Kapp Putsch was an unsuccessful military revolt against the Republican government that took place in mid March 1920—it was followed by several other uprisings by radical elements, however, all these also failed to take hold. The feelings of resentment amongst the German people were further stirred when Upper Silesia was partitioned from Germany and handed over to Poland in 1922. Although reparations payments were temporarily suspended due to the weakness of the economy, by January 1923 the Belgians and French felt that the Germans were dragging their

Hindenburg and Hitler.

heels over restarting the payments. In an attempt to encourage the appearance of more funds, Belgian and French were sent troops into the Ruhr. This created even more bad feeling in the local German population, and the combination of passive resistance and miners' strikes put the economy into meltdown.

Things were going from bad to worse for the German government—in October 1923, Bavaria and Rhineland both declared independence. Hitler felt the time was right to try and seize power, and launched the notorious Beer Hall Putsch in Munich—this attempted coup d'état failed miserably, and Hitler spent 12 months or so in prison. Meanwhile the economy continued to decline—inflation was so high that when devaluation took place, one new Mark was set at the equivalent of one trillion of the old ones. This completely wiped out the savings of Germany's middle and upper classes, something that once again fostered the feelings of anger and resentment. This left the door wide open for political opportunists to make trouble, especially those who could provide excuses to blame others, with the Jews being the favorite target for much of this black propaganda.

When Hitler was released from prison, he decided that he need some effective muscle if he was going to make his way in these troubled times. His solution was to start what was known as the Sturm Abteilung or SA, which translates as Storm Section. They were given uniforms with distinctive brown colored shirts—rather unsurprisingly, they were soon nicknamed simply the "brownshirts." They performed two main functions—firstly to break up the meetings of Hitler's political opponents, and secondly to act as his bodyguard. Many of the recruits to this

Hitler speaks to new recruits of the Hitler Youth and League of German girls (Bund Deutscher Mädel) at the Hall of Heroes in Munich.

Hitler speaking at Blohm & Voss.

Hitler at the Reichsführerschule—*a special school for training future Nazi leaders—at Bernau bei Berlin, just northeast of the capital.*

Hitler and Konstantin Hierl, the Secretary of State for Labour, in front of 47,000 workers of the Reichsarbeitdienst *(Reich Labour Service), Nuremberg*
1935.

organization had previously belonged to the Freikorps, and so were used to the idea of using violence for political ends.

One of the reason that Hitler attracted so much support in this period is that his book Mein Kampf was avidly read by vast numbers of German people. They lapped up suggestions that the German people was of superior stock, and that every cultural, artistic, scientific or technical advancement in human history was almost entirely due to the Aryan race's creative power.

His warnings that the Aryan strain was being polluted by intermarriage with barbarian blood stirred up ill-feeling towards the Jews and Slavs. He'd been blaming the Jews for Germany losing World War I ever since the conflict ended, and in Mein Kampf he claimed that they were trying to control the country by taking over the main political party, the German Social Democrat Party, along with many of the largest companies and several of the country's leading newspapers. Since the Jews owned a large number of the banks and money-lending organizations in Germany, a large proportion of the German population stood to gain financially if the Jews were dispossessed.

Hitler also declared that if he came to power, he would send military forces to occupy Russian land that would then act as a buffer zone for the defence of Germany as well as provide Lebensraum—living space—or the German people.

The situation in Germany was a great worry to the allies, who knew that instability could well lead to war once again. In order to try and kickstart the economy, the Dawes Plan was initiated in 1924—this reduced the reparations burden, and provided large American loans to German companies. Headed by Charles G. Dawes, the plan was initially successful—it slowed the rate of inflation, removed allied troops from the Ruhr, reorganized the German Reichsbank, and lowered the level of reparations for four years. While business started to recover, it soon became apparent that the high level of reparations was not economically sustainable. This provided further fuel for the likes of Hitler who complained that such plans did not lower the overall amount of reparations that Germany had to pay.

In 1925 Ebert died, and Field Marshal Paul von Hindenburg was elected as President of the Republic in his place. The next year Germany was finally admitted to the League of Nations, which was a sign that it was at last being readmitted to the world stage. This was backed up by the Young Plan which replaced the Dawes Plan, and took effect in June 1929; it reduced the massive reparations payments that Germany was committed to. This was the allies way of recognizing that the German economy could not possibly manage to meet its existing obligations and survive.

In the late 1920s Hitler predicted that economic disaster was on its way, but since things were better for the common people than they had been for years, his warnings were laughed at. However, just as it looked as though there was a way out of the gloom for Germany, out of the blue things went from bad to worse with the onset of the Wall Street Crash. This meant that all the American loans given out to German companies were suddenly recalled, which was an absolute disaster, not only for the nation but for the entire European economy. The unexpected downturn left many millions of people with what seemed to be a very bleak future. All of a sudden, Hitler's warnings seemed a lot

Winston Churchill spoke out against appeasement of Nazi Germany during the 1930s.

more sensible than they had previously.

It was in times like these that extremist views tend to be more widely supported, and the Nazi Party was no exception. Vast numbers of people were left jobless as unemployment tripled when companies laid off workers or closed for business. Unemployment rose from 8.5 percent in 1929 to 14 percent in 1930, and then to 21.9 percent in 1931. At its peak it got as high as 29.9 percent in 1932. Hitler's message was popular—he claimed to have the answers that were needed to pull Germany out of economic depression, and the whole population understood that what was needed above all else was a strong leader. These factors combined to sway many voters in his direction, and Hitler did what he could to capitalize on them.

In March 1930, a new minority government was formed after the previous coalition collapsed—composed of elements from the right-wing and center parties, it was led by Heinrich Brüning. This government had to rely on President von Hindenburg's emergency powers, and in an attempt to bolster his position, Brüning called a national election. The people, however, had been polarized by the prevailing economic uncertainty, and both the Nazis and the Communists polled large numbers of votes. During the course of 1931, the German financial situation just got worse and worse. At one stage the entire nation's banks had to close, and things got so bad that America, France and Britain had to give Germany a huge loan.

Since the Nazis were desperate to get their hands on political power, they decided that they should form their own intelligence and security organization. This would give them access to information and secrets that could be used against their opponents, or indeed, against their own members, if need be. This unit was created by Heinrich Himmler in August 1931, and was called the SD or Sicherheitsdienst. Richard Heydrich was appointed as the head of the SD, and it was kept as a distinct unit from the uniformed Schutz Staffel (SS), who were Hitler's personal bodyguard.

Hitler and his entourage enjoyed flexing their muscles by sending the SA in to "sort out" anyone who voiced alternative opinions to those held by the Nazis. As a result, the brownshirts gained a reputation for violence, and since they outnumbered the regular army by four to one, the Chancellor, Heinrich Brüning, feared that they would try to take over the country in a violent coup. In an attempt to allay such fears, he made the SA an illegal organization.

Brüning's main intention was to get the allies to halt Germany's reparations payments by making such drastic budget cuts that the people's suffering would leave no other course of action open. While the ploy succeeded—U.S. president Herbert Hoover finally declared a reparations moratorium in 1932, Brüning had made himself extremely unpopular with the people, and the country teetered on the edge of civil war.

By April 1932, the Nazis had so much popular support that Hitler only just lost out to Hindenburg in the presidential elections. Shortly after this Brüning, who had lost Hindenburg's confidence was replaced by Franz von Papen as German Chancellor. Papen was a member of the Catholic Center Party, who were much more sympathetic to the views held by the Nazis than the SDP had been. In June, Papen's government lifted the ban on the SA or brownshirts, and to the great relief of the entire German people, the allies agreed to end Germany's reparations payments. On top of this, as a result of the latest national elections in July, the Nazis doubled their representation in the Reichstag, greatly improving their political influence. Chancellor Papen did his best to tame Hitler by offering him the job of vice chancellor in his new cabinet, but Hitler was not interested in anything except the chancellorship. This signalled the start of a new phase in the nation's politics.

The presence of a large number of Communist representatives meant that it was not possible for the government to form a constructive coalition, so a further national election was held in November of 1932. This was inconclusive, so things did not get any better. Earlier in the same year Hitler had declared that he would not serve in the German government in any role other than as Chancellor, however, when a new one was appointed it was Major General Kurt von Schleicher who took the role, not Hitler. This infuriated Hitler, and within two months he had managed to convince enough prominent industrialists that a Communist revolution was underway—they in turn put Hindenburg under pressure to make Hitler the Chancellor in place of Schleicher.

Schleicher had been Papen's war minister, and as such was capable of handling the tough situation he could see before him. He realized that Hitler was prepared to use a violent overthrow of the standing government if necessary, and so he tried to convince President Hindenburg that the best course of action would be to dissolve the Reichstag and impose emergency powers. Hindenburg

refused to take a part in such a policy, and in frustration Schleicher resigned.

Hitler knew that the time was right to start bombarding the people with propaganda, and so his master manipulator Joseph Goebbels stepped into action. He instituted a media campaign that went for a blanket coverage of the Nazis main policies. While it was aimed at the disaffected unemployed, it was also designed to appeal to the large numbers of people whose standard of living had declined since the end of World War I. This included everything from farmers to white-collar workers, as well as young people who were attracted to Hitler's strong nationalist ideals.

Throughout this period, the allies had to juggle their priorities carefully. On the one hand they had their own domestic problems to deal with, and the last thing they wanted—or could afford, was to get involved in another conflict with Germany. On the other, they had to field claims of "appeasement" from those who felt that the allies were being too lenient in their dealings with Hitler and his government. Chief amongst these characters was Winston Churchill, who did his best to alert the allies to the threat from Nazi Germany.

Both Britain and France were more or less bankrupted by World War I, and were still trying to recover financially. America had not been affected nearly as badly, but all the same had its hands full with the severe problems caused by the Great Depression. It is not surprising therefore that the allied politicians were doing all they could to deny that Germany posed any kind of military threat.

A further perspective that influenced the allied politicians' thinking was that the appalling conditions in the German domestic economy had generated quite a lot of sympathy around the world. This feeling fostered claims that war reparations had been set at too high a level, and many influential leaders thought that Germany should not have to continue paying up. This was especially true amongst those who were worried about the rise of communism—they felt that Germany was doing a good job of stemming the flow of revolutionary left-wing politics towards the west. As another war loomed, Hitler tested the water by watching the reactions of the allies to his actions in supporting the Spanish Civil War. They demonstrated a "do nothing" policy, which was to have serious repercussions in the very near future.

Hitler meeting and greeting during a journey through East Prussia.

Once he had achieved his aims of becoming chancellor, Hitler began to remove any sign of opposition from potential enemies. The Nazis had a word which described how they intended to go about this—Gleichschaltung, translates as consolidation or synchronization. It was the establishment of a system that controlled and co-ordinated all aspects of society.

The starting point was the elimination of any non-Nazi organizations that could exert influence over the people—these included trade unions and political parties. Even the church did not escape this process—the Nazis established the Ministry of Ecclesiastical Affairs to ensure that no messages came across that could undermine Hitler's work.

When fire destroyed part of the Reichstag building at the end of February 1932, he used this as an excuse to go after many of his enemies. He forced President Hindenburg to issue the Reichstag Fire Decree. This put most human rights on hold, which allowed the Nazis to arrest any political adversaries—particularly the

Communists, and also to let the SA loose to terrorize the voters in the upcoming elections. This wave of violence did not impress many of the German people, and to Hitler's immense annoyance, his party only polled 44 percent of the vote. This was not enough to claim a clear majority, so the Nazis started removing the remaining Communist members either by arresting them on spurious charges, or by terrorizing them so that they went underground. It was not long before the Nazis had eradicated enough of their opposition to rule without hindrance.

In order to give themselves even greater powers, the Enabling Act was passed—this transferred all legislative powers to Hitler's government, which removed the requirement for the Reichstag to approve any legislation passed by the cabinet. It effectively abolished the remainder of the Weimar constitution. With this procedure taken care of, the Nazis banned the Communist and Social Democratic parties. The Third Reich had now legitimized

Delegation from the Saar in front of the Chancellery, Berlin.

Like all political leaders before and since, Hitler spent much time courting the popular vote through walkabouts and visits to hospitals, etc.

itself, and would prove to be unstoppable by anything except military means.

The new government wasted little time in consolidating their bigotries and removing any possible opponents. In April 1933, the "Law for the Restoration of the Professional Civil Service" started a purge from the service of all Jews, Communists and other people considered to be any kind of a threat to the regime. This was backed up a month later by making the Nazis the only legal political party—all the others were closed down.

In order to stimulate the economy, the Nazis instituted the first Reinhardt Plan—this was a massive attempt to reduce unemployment and return the country to prosperity through government spending. The money—one billion Reichsmarks, was spent in two major ways; one of these was on large-scale public works such as housing, motorways and bridges. The other was on rearmament—many of the unemployed were absorbed into the

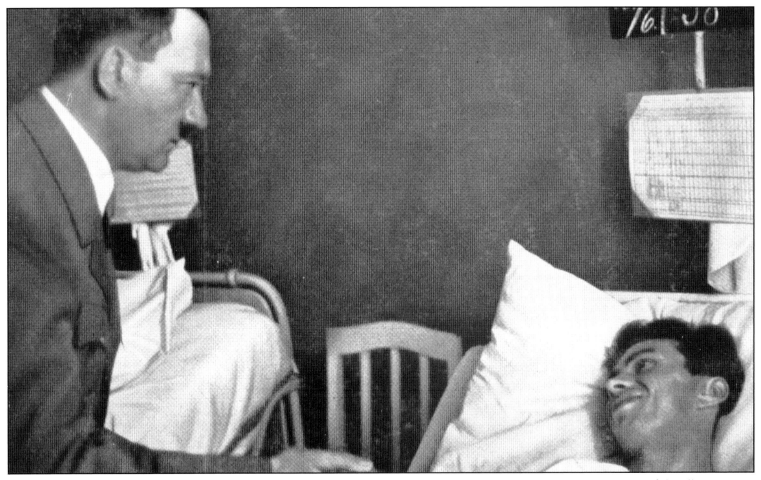

Hitler on a visit to a hospital.

army, and huge sums were spent on military equipment. A second Reinhardt Plan added another half billion Reichsmarks later the same year.

While the plans succeeded in increasing the country's prosperity, many of the methods used to raise the money were not sustainable—the government printed large amounts of extra currency, and used highly dubious financing deals to create new armaments companies. In order to hide the scale of rearmament, the government stopped the publication of data concerning the national budget in 1934. To the great concern of the allies, not only was Germany in the process of rearming, it also withdrew from the Disarmament Conference and the League of Nations. Conscious of these feelings, Hitler tried to convince the world that he only had peaceful intentions, and signed a non-aggression treaty with Poland. This was a two-edged sword—not only did it serve to allay fears of future German aggression, it also undermined attempts by the allies to build up military alliances and defences.

At this time Hitler also had some significant domestic

Another huge rally greets their leader.

The Reichstag—the German parliament—burns on the night of February 27, 1933. From its ashes would rise Hitler's Third Reich.

problems to deal with. Although the SA had been legitimized by Papen's government in June 1932, their time had come. Until then Hitler had manipulated them to his own ends, using the band of thugs to murder, terrorize and threaten anyone who stood in the way of the Nazi Party. The leader of the SA, Ernst Röhm had ambitions that threatened Hitler—he wanted, for instance, to overthrow the regular army so that the SA could become the dominant military force. It certainly was large enough—while the regular army numbered only 100,000 (the maximum it was allowed under the Treaty of Versailles), the SA numbered more than 400,000. This idea did not fit in with Hitler's master plan, however, and with the encouragement of Hermann Göring (who commanded the Prussian Gestapo and was Röhm's arch rival), he ordered the Himmler's SS to massacre the leaders of the SA—including Röhm, who was on old friend of Hitler's. This infamous event became known as the Night of the Long Knives.

With the SA out of the way, Himmler reorganized the SS to turn it into one of the largest and most powerful organizations in Germany. To do this he knew that his recruits would have to be well-disciplined and fanatically loyal, unlike the drunken thugs of the SA. To attract the best people, Himmler created an elitist image by the use of distinct black uniforms and special insignia. Himmler made the SS swear allegiance to Adolf Hitler, with the motto My honor is loyalty—this was a clever move, since it made Hitler feel comfortable that the SS existed with the aim of furthering his ambitions, and no one else's. It gave Himmler an enormous amount of power, and the SS became the backbone of the Nazi party.

Hitler speaking at Nuremberg.

In 1934, Hitler's cabinet was composed of the following members:

Position	Position (translated)	Name	Years in Office
Führer und Reichskanzler	Führer & Chancellor	Adolf Hitler	1934–1945
Reichsarbeitsminister	Minister of Labour	Franz Seldte	1933–1945
Reichsaußenminister	Minister for Foreign Affairs	Konstantin von Neurath	1932–1938
Reichsfinanzminister	Minister of Finances	Lutz Schwerin von Krosigk	1933–1945
Reichsjustizminister	Minister of Justice	Franz Gürtner	1933–1941
Reichsminister des Innern	Minister of Interior	Wilhelm Frick	1933–1943
Reichsminister für Ernährung und Landwirtschaft	Minister of Agriculture	Walther Darré	1933–1943
Reichsminister für Luftfahrt	Minister of Air	Hermann Göring	1933–1945
Reichsminister für Volksaufklärung und Propaganda	Minister for Public Enlightenment and Propaganda	Joseph Goebbels	1933–1945
Reichsminister für Wissenschaft, Erziehung und Volksbildung	Minister for Science, Education and Culture	Bernhard Rust	1934–1945
Reichsverkehrs- und Reichspostminister	Minister of Post and Communication	Paul Freiherr von Eltz-Rübenach	1933–1937
Reichswehrminister	Minister of Defence	Werner von Blomberg	1933–1938
Reichswirtschaftsminister	Minister of Economics	Hjalmar Schacht	1933–1937

Hitler and Hjalmar Schacht at the laying of the foundation stone for the new Reichsbank, May 5, 1934. Schacht was Minister of Economics 1933–37.

The racial purity card was something that the Nazis had been playing since the early 1930's, and Himmler was responsible for implementing many of the relevant policies. In 1931 he formed the Race and Resettlement Central Office, which was also known as RUSHA—its purpose was check that all SS men were racially pure, since Himmler believed that his men were the basis of a new Nordic master race. All new SS recruits had to show paper records proving that they had no Jewish, Slavic, or other "undesirable" blood lines as far back as 1750. This also included checks to ensure that they had no genetic medical issues or mental health problems. Since the idea was to create a new race composed entirely of pure Aryan children, any prospective SS wives also had to go through the same checking procedures.

In August 1934, President von Hindenburg died—this gave Hitler the chance to assume the Presidency as well as the Chancellorship. In order to legitimize the move, he organized a national vote, but in doing so he also ensured that no one was able to voice any public disapproval of the idea. With no contrary messages to consider, the German public supported Hitler with 88 percent of the vote in his favor. In order to form a successful government, the Nazis created an alliance with the conservatives—in the short-term, this suited Hitler's agenda, but their period of usefulness would prove to be short-lived.

With the matter of political control out of the way, Hitler became a lot more brazen in his actions. In 1935 he disregarded the disarmament clauses of the Versailles Treaty and stepped up the process of rearmament. The allies could see that Germany was growing powerful once again, and Britain's politicians tried to deal with this by signing various accords with her. This was labelled as "appeasement" by those who were opposed to standing by and allowing Germany to rearm. Foremost among such people were politicians like Winston Churchill, who mistrusted Hitler from the start.

A further tightening of the Nazis grip on power occurred in June 1936 when Himmler was appointed to the position of Chief of the German Police—he then divided the system into two distinct divisions. The first was called the Ordnungspolizei, and was made up of regular uniformed police, whilst the second—and more sinister section, was called the Sicherheitspolizei, or Security police. This unit included the Gestapo, and was run by Himmler's number two—the brutal Reinhard Heydrich.

In 1936 the Nazis stepped up pressure on the Jews by enacting the Nuremberg Laws which deprived them of their citizenship rights. For many people of Jewish origin this was the last straw, and large numbers of them left the country to seek friendlier climes. If this wasn't enough to alert the allies to Hitler's true intentions, he then sent troops into the demilitarized Rhineland in clear violation of the Versailles and Locarno Treaties.

When Germany annexed Austria in spring 1938, the Nazis began systematically expelling the large numbers of Jews from the country. Although the rich could afford to pay for travel to friendlier shores, the poorer elements could not. In order to

Hitler and his cabinet.

Hitler at a motor show in Berlin, 1935.

Hitler greeted by his adoring countrymen, Bückeberg 1935.

Hitler applauds Wilhelm Furtwängler, the conductor of the Berlin Philharmonic Orchestra.

Hjalmar Schacht resigned as Minister of Economics in 1937 and as Reichsbank President in 1939. Imprisoned after the July Bomb Plot he was lucky to survive the war. On trial at Nuremberg, he was found not guilty of war crimes.

Hitler lays the foundations of the meeting house in the Adolf-Hitler-Koog, reclaimed land in Dithmarschen on the North Sea coast of Schleswig-Holstein.

Hitler greets youthful workers at the Chancellery on May 1, 1934, National Labour Day.

organize their expulsion, the Nazis set up the "Central Office of Jewish Emigration" in Vienna. This was run by Adolf Eichmann, who ran the system there very smoothly and efficiently—he was known to his peers as the "Jewish Specialist." He extorted large sums of money from the richer members of the Jewish community to pay for exit visas for the poor. Within 18 months, he had reduced the Jewish population in Austria by half. Eichmann's example was extremely highly regarded within the Nazi party, and it was not long before "Offices of Jewish Emigration" were established throughout the German Reich.

The Nazis hatred of the Jews continued to build, and in late 1938, things got a lot worse after what is known as the "Night of broken glass." or Kristallnacht. This marked the start of a campaign of violent persecution—synagogues and other Jewish properties were burnt, and thousands of Jews were beaten up and arrested.

Education

Hitler loved architecture: here he is seen with Professors Troost and Wackerle studying a model in Munich.

Adoring crowds greet Hitler as he leaves the House of German Art in Munich.

Hitler acknowledges the crowd during the Bayreuth festival.

And this is the Bayreuth crowd!

Another view of Hitler at the 1935 Berlin Motor Show.

Hitler and Dr. Robert Ley, head of the German Labour Front, during the 1935 Nuremberg Rally.

A major part of the success of the Nazi party must be attributed to the manner in which they indoctrinated their youth through a targeted education system. Hitler was under no illusions as to the usefulness of intellectual subjects. He stated that: "Knowledge is ruin to my young men. A violent, active, dominating, brutal youth—that is what I am after." He also said that, "The German youth of the future must be swift like the greyhound, tough like leather, and hard like Krupp steel." In order to achieve this, an education system was established that ensured that Germany's young minds were filled with propaganda driven ideals of honor and patriotism for the Fatherland.

The Nazis forced all teachers to join the National Socialist Teachers League, and in doing so and they had to swear an oath to "be loyal and obedient to Adolf Hitler." No Jewish teachers were

Hitler on a factory visit receives the "German Greeting".

allowed to keep their posts, and if there was any doubt about their loyalty they were dismissed. Special schools were set up for Jewish children, who were no longer allowed to attend mainstream German schools. The racial divide was further enforced with the inclusion of "Racial Sciences" into the school curriculum. This was designed to indoctrinate children into the idea that the German people were genetically superior to Jewish and others of mixed blood. This concept was extended right across the board of educational subjects—history lessons were changed to lectures on Hitler's life, and in maths lessons instead of counting oranges and apples, examples were based on bombs and craters.

Manipulating the minds of children while they were at school wasn't enough for Hitler though. He wanted to toughen them up physically as well—and felt they should join militarized youth organizations. As a result the Hitlerjugend, or Hitler Youth was formed in June 1933—this was run by Baldur von Schirach, who made it into one of the largest groups of its kind in the world. Based on existing youth groups, it focused on physical activities such as sports and living rough in the outdoors, with camping and hiking trips being especially favored. The organization differed from the others in that if featured lectures on patriotism and taught boys how to become fighters.

Propaganda

Adolf Hitler was a great believer in the use of propaganda. Not only did he devote two chapters of Mein Kampf to the subject, but he saw to it that his ideas were put into practice wholesale. The Nazi Party soon worked out the best ways to deliver their messages, and they exploited the various media to the full. Hitler used propaganda as a tool of manipulation of the masses, and was not interested in reaching what he saw as the relatively small numbers of more highly educated people. He therefore targeted his campaigns at simple emotions, rather than the intellect. Repetition of the basic message was a key factor, and short slogans were used whenever possible.

The basic principle was that they would start with ideological indoctrination, and to this end they employed mass rallies, meetings, billboards and, of course, through the radio and via film theatres. In the early days of the Third Reich, they simply wanted to attract attention to themselves, but as time went on they had specific messages to convey. These included reinforcing the regime's ideals and increasing its popularity with the masses.

From the very earliest days, Hitler realized that "truth" as a concept was irrelevant. If the message was put across properly, people could be made to believe almost anything—especially if they wanted to. As a consequence, Nazi propaganda was full of half-truths, false facts, innuendo and absolute lies. They wove clever webs of deception to justify their political aims and intended military actions. They ruthlessly exploited the widely-held resentment of the humiliation wrought on the German

Hitler visits the Bavarian State Library.

Hitler at shipbuilders Blohm & Voss.

Hitler greeted by German girls.

The opening of the autobahn between Frankfurt and Darmstadt in 1935. From left to right: von Blomberg (Minister of Defence), Hitler, Dr. Todt (head of Organisation Todt, the unit set up in 1938 to build military installations and autobahns suitable for military use), Dr. Schacht (president of Reichsbank), Dr. Dorpmüller (director of German railways), Goebbels.

Hitler looks over the Rhine at Bad Godesberg on September 24, 1938, during the negotiations with Neville Chamberlain over Czechoslovakia.

people by the Versailles Treaty, and used this to stir up enthusiasm for Nazi ideology.

One of the principle targets for Nazi propaganda was to stir up hatred for the Jews. Since a key element of Hitler's philosophy was that the people should only have one enemy to focus on, he ensured that all the country's problems were blamed directly on "The Jew." As a result he stirred up racist sentiment wherever and whenever he could. His aim was to instil in the German people a hatred of anything and everything associated with the Jews, so that they could be persuaded to believe that the country should be rid of the "Jewish Pest." As part of this process he made sure that anti-Semitic films were shown regularly in the cinemas. Out of sight of the public, however, he ensured that his movie makers also made fake films that showed how well the Jews were being treated in the concentration camps. These movies were never intended for consumption by the home market, but were aimed squarely at silencing complaints from around the world. From Hitler's point of view they proved effective at keeping foreign governments from interfering in his policies.

The use of propaganda was so important to the Third Reich that a large amount of resources were channelled into ensuring that it was exploited to the full. The centre of operations became the Reich Ministry of Public Enlightenment and Propaganda, which was established on March 5, 1933, under the control of Joseph Goebbels. The ministry had seven departments; these were:

administration and organization, propaganda, radio, the press, films, theatre, and adult education—this included all forms of literature.

Hitlerjugend drummers at the 1935 Nuremberg Rally: 54,000 youths attended.

Electioneering in 1932.

All children joined either the Hitlerjugend *or* Bund Deutscher Mädel *when they reached the age of 14/15—so long as their ancestry was "pure".*

In important instrument in the manipulation of the people was through the use of public holidays to celebrate events that were of particular significance to the Third Reich. These included:

January 30—Day of the Seizure of Power (Machergreifung)

The first of the many Third Reich public holidays held throughout the year was celebrated on January 30. This occasion was to mark the anniversary of Adolf Hitler being elected Kanzler or chancellor on January 30, 1933.

February 24—Foundation Day of the NSDAP (Parteigründungsfeier)

To keep the importance of the Nazi Party fresh in the minds of the populace, a national holiday was established to mark the anniversary of its foundation. Although the National Socialist German Workers' Party (NSDAP) was actually named on April 1, 1920, the Nazis chose to celebrate February 24, 1920 as the day on which it was actually founded.

March 16—National Day of Mourning (Heldengedenktag)

A public holiday had traditionally been held every year to mourn those killed in military action, and was customarily on the fifth Sunday before Easter. Although it was originally associated with the care and upkeep of the cemeteries the servicemen and women had been buried in, the Nazis decided to take it over for their own ends. It was instead marked each year on March 16, and

was renamed Heroes' Remembrance Day in the process.

April 20—Hitler's Birthday (Führergeburtstag)

The Nazis decided that celebrating the Führer's birthday with a public holiday would be an excellent way of ensuring that he would be remembered across the nation. Since Adolf Hitler was born on April 20, 1889, this was the day of the holiday. It was marked with the display of large numbers of red, white and black flags and pennants, as well as millions of photographs of the Führer. Long ceremonies were also held—these often incorporated torch-light parades, mass choirs and initiations. The date, however, also had deeper meaning to those who were involved in the Pagan ritual of Leader worship—this included many of the leading Nazi Party members, including such important characters as Himmler.

May 1—National Labor Day (Nationaler Feiertag des Deutschen Volkes)

Although May 1 was traditionally perceived as a socialist holiday, the Nazis had no problem with altering it to suit their own ends. Instead of celebrating the rights of the worker, it was turned into a pseudo-Pagan festival, with parades, May-pole dances and huge bonfires. In many ways it was quite close to the original May 1 event that had been celebrated for hundreds of years by the true Pagans (to whom it was known as Beltaine), well before the socialists had usurped it for their own political reasons.

May—Mothering Sunday (Muttertag)

The Third Reich wanted its Aryan population to produce lots of children, and so the second Sunday in May was designated as Mothering Sunday. It was intended to honor those women who had raised several good German children. Crosses of honor were presented to prolific mothers at mass public ceremonies, reinforcing the message that babies were good for the nation.

Summer Solstice (Sommersonnenwende)

The Day of the Summer Solstice, June 21, was celebrated with large public bonfires where wreathes commemorating war heroes or Nazi Party martyrs were thrown into the flames. The observers then jumped through the flames, lit torches from the fires and finally joined a long procession home. At these events Party officials would often make political speeches to rouse up particular sentiments—these were known as "fire speeches" or Feuerspruche. In 1938, the Summer Solstice was celebrated on a mountain—the Hesselberg, that Adolf Hitler had declared to be sacred to the German people. A huge fire had been built, but before it was lit Julius Streicher, a prominent Nazi Party member stood in front of the assembled throng and told them that:

"We Germans have no need of men in black to whom to make our confessions in order that we might be strengthened for the coming year; we have become our own priests; let us throw our sins into these holy flames that we might descend from the mountain with souls cleansed!"

September—Reich Party Rally (Reichsparteitage)

One of the most important public holidays as far as the Nazis were concerned was a huge three-day festival held to celebrate the Third Reich every year in the old city of Nürnberg. It began with a rally where massed throngs marched past the Führer, after which he gave them a rousing speech. The whole area was bedecked with flags, pennants, and giant posters, and loud music was played through large public address systems. There were also lots of parades, mass choirs, and other events designed to instil in the people feelings of patriotism towards the Fatherland and hatred towards the Nazis number one enemy – "The Jew."

Autumn—Harvest Thanksgiving Day (Erntedanktag)

Since a large part of the German population was reliant to a greater or lesser extent on agriculture, the autumn harvest was an important time to a lot of people. Hitler's propagandists therefore made sure that the festivals which were traditionally held at harvest-time were directly associated with the Nazi Party. They set aside a day to pay tribute to the German farmer.

November 9—Anniversary of the Beer-Hall Putsch (Gedenktag für die Gefallenen der Bewegung)

The deaths of the Munich Beer-Hall Putsch martyrs were commemorated every year on November 9. This national holiday was to remember those who died as well as the survivors of the failed attempt to start a revolution in Munich on November

9, 1923. Although events were held across Germany by every individual Nazi group, the main ceremony was held in Munich, where there were grand re-enactments of the martyr's march through the streets of Munich to the Feldherrnhalle. This was where the National Socialist movement had been 'sanctified in blood' by the loss of 16 lives. To many party members it was the most 'holy' celebration of the year as they considered the deaths to have been brave sacrifices by fallen heroes. The event was also seen as an occasion to celebrate the ancestors of German people who had given life to the Aryan race. In order to ensure that the most was made of this event, the Nazi Party published detailed guidelines in a periodical called Die neue Gemeinschaft.

Winter—Day of the Winter Solstice (Wintersonnenwende)

December 21 was the Day of the Winter Solstice, an occasion which was also referred to as Yuletide. Its significance was that it was not based on the birth of Christ, but rather as a celebration of the rising of the "Sun Child" at the winter solstice. It was therefore another Pagan-based festival, and Nazi propagandists declared it was holy to the ancestors of the German people. The Nordic-inspired event saw gifts being exchanged "without any thought of Christian rewards being reaped in heaven," and was therefore a way of expressing "Germanic love, Germanic ways and Germanic benevolence."

December 24—Christmas (Volksweinacht)

The Nazis did their best to replace Christmas with the Day of

the Winter Solstice. Their propaganda made it clear that it had not been invented by the Christians, but was in fact first held by their Germanic forefathers at the solstice. Goebbels wanted to get rid of Christmas altogether as he considered it to drain the resources of the war effort, and that it was "overly sentimental" and thus weakened the German psyche.

Breeding Racial Purity

Since the Nazis believed they were starting a Thousand-Year Reich, they wanted to ensure a plentiful supply of racially pure "Nordic" children. Himmler was particularly preoccupied with this, and told his SS men that they should, "Show that you are ready, through your faith in the Führer and for the sake of the life of our blood and people, to regenerate life for Germany just as bravely as you know how to fight and die for Germany." He told them that they should have at least four children, and that they should not only make their wives pregnant, but any other "racially pure" women as well—this would not be adultery as it was in the nation's best interests.

The concept was carried forward in other ways as well—special maternity units were set up for unmarried mothers to give birth. Called "Spring of Life" (Lebensborn) homes, generally were places that had been confiscated from wealthy Jews. Those women who did not want to keep their babies were able to have them adopted by SS families, and special accolades were given to mothers who produced four or more children.

Racial Cleansing

In stark contrast to Himmler's interest in the fostering of German babies, he ordered his SS men to commit acts of barbarism on those he considered to be "subhuman" in a reign of terror throughout the occupied territories. Anyone though to be Jewish, Slavic or communist was seen as an enemy, and therefore fair game to SS brutality.

The allies were well aware of what was going on, and in 1940 Clement Attlee gave a speech in the House of Commons, in which he said, "We are now faced with the danger of the world relapsing into barbarism. Nazism is the outstanding menace to civilization, not only because of the character and actions of the men who are in absolute control of a great nation, but because of their ideas which are openly in conflict with all the conceptions upon which civilized life is based."

In 1941, Hitler ordered the physical extermination of the Jews—this was to be called the Endlösung—the Final Solution. Heydrich and Eichmann were tasked with implementing this new wave of atrocities. Instead of permitting Jews to emigrate, they were to be shipped to concentration camps where they would be killed in special killing centers. These were to be well away from the scrutiny of the western world, hidden in the depths of the eastern Germany Reich. Eichmann would take control of transporting the Jews to the camps, and would co-ordinate the capabilities of each killing center to optimize their efficiency.

One of the problems that such a plan posed was just how they would kill such large numbers of people quickly and cheaply. Eichmann discussed this with Rudolf Hoss, the commandant of Auschwitz, which was the largest of the concentration camps. Together they decided that a potassium cyanide gas that was widely used as a rat poison—Zyklon B—was the most suitable agent.

The Final Solution needed the complicity of many leading Nazis, and to ensure that they all toed the line, Reinhard Heydrich and Adolf Eichmann organized the Wannsee Conference in 1942. Wannsee was a plush suburb of Berlin, and was a most unlikely setting for a meeting that was intended to co-ordinate the killing of 11 million innocent people. It was entitled the "Final Solution to the Jewish Question," and it gained the support of all those who attended.

Knowing he had unquestioning support, Eichmann methodically organized just how he was going to move so many people out of their homes and move them across large distances to the various concentration camps. Officially they were told that they were being resettled in the east—this was not only to keep them from panicking and trying to escape, but it also ensured the support of the common German people. Fake propaganda films were made showing the Jews being moved into comfortable homes and enjoying their new lifestyle, and so little resistance was felt.

The ethnic cleansing was done in a rigorous "area by area" manner, with the Jews being told to take their belongings and wait at predetermined locations to join a train. Once there, they were put into over-crowded boxcars, with no food, water or toilets. If this was not bad enough, the trains did not stop for several days, and large numbers of people died from starvation, dehydration and illness. Eichmann was responsible for the transportation a many millions of people—these included not just Jews, but also Poles, Czechs, Russians, gypsies, communists and other "undesirables." Even though the vast majority of these people died in the killing centers, after the war had ended Eichmann refused to take any responsibility, saying that he was just "obeying orders" from his superiors.

A large number of those shipped to the concentration camps were used as slave labor—this could be anything from work in armaments factories to mining—it could even be involved in running the killing "ovens" where countless numbers of people lost their lives. Conditions were so bad for the slave workers that huge numbers of them died from malnutrition, exhaustion and disease. Others were executed for the slightest infringement of camp rules. The factories that used these workers made complaints to Himmler that the workers were dying faster than they could be replaced, and in the interests of German armaments production, conditions were improved enough to reduce the death rate. Himmler himself stated that:

"What happens to a Russian, to a Czech, does not interest me in the slightest...Whether nations live in prosperity or starve to death like cattle interests me only in so far as we need them as slaves to our culture; otherwise it is of no interest to me. Whether 10,000 Russian females fall down from exhaustion while digging an antitank ditch interests me only in so far as the antitank ditch for Germany is finished."

Himmler's stated lack of concern for the fate of slave laborers was not merely verbal—a witness who saw conditions at the Krupp Works which produced armaments said that:

"The clothing of the Eastern workers was likewise completely inadequate. They worked and slept in the same clothing in which they had arrived from the East. Virtually all of them had no overcoats and were compelled to use their blankets as coats in the cold and rainy weather. In view of the shortage of shoes many workers were forced to go to work in their bare feet even in winter... The sanitary conditions were atrocious. At Kramerplatz only ten children's toilets were available for 1,200 inhabitants...The Tartars and Kirghiz suffered the most; they collapsed like flies from bad housing, insufficient food, overwork, and insufficient rest. These workers were likewise afflicted with spotted fever. Lice, the carrier of the disease, together with the countless fleas, bugs & other vermin tortured the inhabitants of these camps."

While conditions were improved enough to maintain the supply of workers needed to keep the munitions factories open, the casualty figures were still appalling. Deaths occurred from malnutrition, disease and beatings right up to the end of the war. Even then, the toll still continued as a result of injuries sicknesses, and of those who survived, many were so traumatized by their experiences that they never fully recovered.

This poster urged a Yes vote on one of the four referendums Hitler called during the 1930's.

Bayrisches-Central=
Landwirtschaftsfest
Ausstellungen:
Landwirtschaft
Gewerbe
Jagdu.Fischerei

16.September
bis
1.Oktober
München1933

A 1933 poster announcing an agricultural fair. It's eight months after Hitler took power, and the Swastika is showing up everywhere.

This visual from the mid-1930's shows Germany in white, with the 100,000-man army permitted by the Treaty of Versailles, surrounded by heavily armed neighbors.

Through military will to military strength.

In the deepest need Hindenburg chose Adolf Hitler for Reich Chancellor. You too should vote for List 1.

The Führer promised to motorize Germany. In 1932, 104,000 motor vehicles were manufactured, 33,000 people were employed, and goods with a total value of 295,000,000 marks were produced. In 1935, 353,000 vehicle.

This poster promotes Hitler's book Mein Kampf, announcing that four million copies have been sold.

Germans buy German goods The bottom text translates German Week German Goods German Labor. Germans buy German goods The bottom text translates German Week German Goods German Labor.

Hitler is building. Help him. Buy German goods.

1935 — Saar Referendum! We in the Saar are loyal — We stand for honor and the Fatherland. Are you thinking of us.

All Germany hears the Führer on the People's Receiver.

This poster links the German Labor Front (the DAF) to World War I. The point is that just as soldiers were comrades regardless of their standing in civil life, so too all German workers were comrades in the DAF.

Unshakable, determined to fight, certain of victory.

Youth Serves the Führer. All 10-year-olds into the Hitler Youth. Membership in the Hitler Youth had become mandatory in 1936.

Adolf Hitler's youth attends community schools.

Mothers! Fight for your children.

Says one can join at 18, and sign up for shorter or longer periods of service. It gives the address of the recruiting office in Munich.

The guarantee of German military strength.

January 1933-1943. One Battle! One Victory.

Long live Germany.

CHRONOLOGY OF WORLD WAR II

1938	
March 11	Anschluss — German annexation of Austria.
September 29	Munich Agreement signed.
October 5	Germany occupies Sudetenland.

1939	
March 14	Slovakia declares its independence.
March 31	Britain and France give guarantee to Poland.
April 7	Italy invades Albania.
May 22	Germany and Italy sign Pact of Steel.
August 23	Molotov-Ribbentrop pact signed between Germany and the Soviet Union.
September 1	Germany invades Poland.
September 1	Britain and France declare war on Germany.
September 17	Soviet Union invades Poland.
November 30	Soviet Union at war with Finland.

1940	
March 12	War between Soviet Union and Finland ends.
April 9	Germany invades Norway and Denmark.
April 14	Allied troops land in Norway.
May 10	Fall Gelb, the offensive in the West, is launched by Germany.
May 10	Churchill becomes Prime Minister of Great Britain.
May 14	Dutch Army surrenders.
May 26	Beginning of evacuation of Dunkirk.
May 28	Belgium surrenders.
June 2	Allies withdraw from Norway.
June 4	Dunkirk evacuation complete.
June 10	Italy declares war on Britain and France.
June 14	Germans enter Paris.
June 21	Italy launches offensive against France.
June 22	France and Germany sign armistice.
June 24	France and Italy sign armistice.
July 3	Royal Navy attacks French fleet at Mers el Kebir.
July 10	Beginning of the Battle of Britain.
September 17	Operation Sealion (the invasion of England) postponed by Hitler.
September 21	Italy and Germany sign Tripartite Pact.
September 27	Japan signs Tripartite Pact.
November 20	Hungary signs Tripartite Pact.
November 22	Romania signs Tripartite Pact.
November 23	Slovakia signs Tripartite Pact.

1941	
January 19	British launch East African campaign offensive.
January 22	Australian troops take Tobruk.
February 6	British capture Benghazi.
February 11	Rommel arrives in Libya.

March 25	Yugoslavia signs Tripartite Pact.
March 27	Yugoslavia leaves Tripartite Pact after coup d'etat.
March 28	Successful British naval action against Italians off Cape Matapan.
April 6–8	Axis forces invade Yugoslavia and Greece.
April 11	U.S.A. extends its naval neutrality patrols.
April 13	Belgrade falls to Axis forces.
April 14	Yugoslav forces surrender.
April 22	Greek First Army surrenders at Metsovan Pass.
May 16	Italians surrender to British at Amba Alagi.
May 20	Germans land on Crete.
May 24	H.M.S. Hood sunk by Bismarck.
May 27	Bismarck sunk by Royal Navy.
June 1	British withdraw from Crete.
June 2	Germany launches Operation Barbarossa against the Soviet Union.
July 27	Japanese troops invade French Indo-China.
September 19	Germans capture Kiev.
September 28	Three-power Conference in Moscow.
December 6	Britain declares war on Finland, Hungary and Rumania.
December 7	Japanese attack Pearl Harbor.
December 8	U.S.A. and Britain declare war on Japan.
December 8	Japanese invade Malaya and Thailand.
December 11	Germany and Italy declare war on the U.S.A.
December 14	Japanese begin invasion of Burma.
December 25	Japanese take Hong Kong.
1942	
February 15	Japanese troops capture Singapore from British.
February 27	Battle of the Java Sea.
February 28	Japanese invade Java.
March 8	Japanese invade New Guinea.
March 17	General MacArthur appointed to command South-West Pacific.
April 9	U.S. troops surrender in Bataan.
April 16	George Cross awarded to Island of Malta by H.R.H. King George VI.
April 26	Anglo-Soviet Treaty signed.
May 6	Japanese take Corregidor.
May 7	Battle of the Coral Sea.
May 20	British troops withdraw from Burma.
May 26	Rommel's Afrika Korps attack British at Gazala.
May 30	Royal Air Force launches first thousand-bomber raid on Germany.
June 4	Battle of Midway.
June 21	Rommel's Afrika Korps take Tobruk.
July 1	Sevastopol taken by Germans.
July 1	First Battle of El Alamein.
August 7	U.S. troops land on Guadalcanal.
August 11	PEDESTAL convoy arrives in Malta.
August 19	Raid on Dieppe.

August 31	Battle of Alam Halfa.
October 24	Second Battle of El Alamein.
November 8	Operation TORCH landings in North Africa.
November 11	Germans and Italians occupy Vichy France.
November 27	French fleet scuttled at Toulon.
1943	
January 14–24	Allied Conference at Casablanca.
January 23	British troops take Tripoli.
February 2	Germans surrender at Stalingrad.
February 8	Red Army captures Kursk.
February 13	Chindits launch first operation into Burma.
February 19	Battle for the Kasserine Pass.
April 19	First Warsaw rising.
April 19	Bermuda Conference.
May 11–25	TRIDENT conference in Washington.
May 13	Axis forces surrender in North Africa.
May 16	Royal Air Force "Dambuster" raid on Mohne and Eder dams.
May 24	U-boats withdraw from North Atlantic.
July 5	Battle of Kursk.
July 10	Allies land in Sicily.
July 25	Mussolini resigns.
September 3	Allies land on Italian mainland.
September 8	Surrender of Italy announced.
September 9	Allies land at Salerno.
September 10	Germans occupy Rome and Northern Italy.
October 13	Italy declares war on Germany.
November 6	Red Army captures Kiev.
November	First Allied conference in Cairo. 23–26
November 28–December 1	Allied conference in Teheran.
December 3–7	Second Allied conference in Cairo.
December 24	General Eisenhower promoted to supreme commander for OVERLORD, the Normandy landings.
1944	
January 22	Allies land at Anzio.
January 27	Red Army raises Siege of Leningrad.
January 31	U.S. forces land on Marshall Islands.
February 1	Battle for Monte Cassino begins.
March 2	Second Chindit operation into Burma.
May 11	Fourth Battle of Monte Cassino.
June 4	U.S. troops enter Rome.
June 6	Operation OVERLORD — Allied landings in Normandy.
June 19	Battle of the Philippine Sea.
July 1	Breton Woods conference.
July 20	Failed attempt to assassinate Hitler — July Bomb plot.
August 1	Second Warsaw rising.
August 4	Allied troops enter Florence.

August 15	Operation DRAGOON — Allied landings in southern France.
August 25	Germans in Paris surrender.
September 4	British troops capture Antwerp.
September	OCTAGON — Allied conference at Quebec. 12–16
September 17	Operation MARKET GARDEN at Arnhem.
September 21	Dumbarton Oaks conference.
October 14	British enter Athens.
October 23	De Gaulle recognised by Britain and U.S.A. as head of French Provisional Government.
October 24	Battle of Leyte Gulf.
December 16	Germans launch campaign in the Ardennes.
1945	
January 4–13	Japanese Kamikaze planes sink 17 U.S. ships and damage 50 more.
January 14	Red Army advances into East Prussia.
January 17	Red Army takes Warsaw.
January 30–February 3	First ARGONAUT Allied conference at Malta.
February 4–11	Second ARGONAUT Allied conference at Malta.
February 6	Allies clear Colmar pocket.
February 19	U.S. forces land on Iwo Jima.
February 26	U.S. 9th Army reaches Rhine.
March 7	U.S. 3rd Army crosses Rhine at Remagen Bridge.
March 20	British capture Mandalay.
March 30	Red Army enters Austria.
April 1	U.S. First and Ninth Armies encircle the Ruhr.
April 1	U.S. forces land on Okinawa.
April 12	President Roosevelt dies and Truman becomes president.
April 13	Red Army takes Vienna.
April 25	U.S. and Soviet forces meet at Torgau.
April 28	Mussolini shot by partisans.
April 29	Germans sign surrender terms for troops in Italy.
April 30	Hitler commits suicide.
May 2	Red Army takes Berlin.
May 3	British enter Rangoon.
May 4	German forces in the Netherlands, northern Germany and Denmark surrender to General Montgomery on Luneburg Heath.
May 5	Germans in Norway surrender.
May 7	General Alfred Jodl signs unconditional surrender of Germany at Reims, to take effect on May 9.
May 8	Victory in Europe Day.
May 10	Red Army takes Prague.
July 17–August 2	Allied TERMINAL conference held in Potsdam.
July 26	Winston Churchill resigns after being defeated in the general election. Clement Attlee becomes Prime Minister of Great Britain.
August 6	Atomic bomb dropped on Hiroshima.
August 8	Soviet Union declares war on Japan.
August 9	Atomic bomb dropped on Nagasaki.
August 14	Unconditional surrender of Japanese forces announced by Emperor Hirohito.
August 15	Victory in Japan Day.
September 2	Japanese sign surrender aboard U.S.S. Missouri in Tokyo Bay.